Endorsements

"In today's chaotic and fast-moving world, *The Gratitude and Glimmers Journal* helps you tune into the small moments of joy, beauty, and meaning—because even in uncertainty, there is always a glimmer to be found."

—Ilona Pamplona, author of *Human Design Made Easy: Understanding the Five Energy Types*

"*The Gratitude and Glimmers Journal* is the perfect daily reminder to live with more purpose, intention, and joy. A daily anchor to make room for the people and things that matter most."

—Shira Gill, author of *Minimalista: Your Step-by-Step Guide to a Better Home, Wardrobe, and Life*

The GRATITUDE *and* GLIMMERS JOURNAL

Books by the Author

Raising Anti-Diet Kids: A Parent's Actionable Guide to Ditch Diets and Cultivate Body Respect (2023)

The GRATITUDE *and* GLIMMERS JOURNAL

Andrea Dow

ONE IDEA PRESS

Published by One Idea Press LLC and Books That Save Lives, an Imprint of Jim Dandy, Publishing LLC

Cover Design: Elina Diaz
Cover Photo/Illustration: Elina Diaz
Layout & Design: Elina Diaz

Jim Dandy Publishing
6252 Peach Avenue
Van Nuys, CA 91411

info@jimdandypublishing.com

For bulk orders, special quantities, course adoptions, and corporate sales, please email info@jimdandypublishing.com

The Gratitude and Glimmers Journal

Library of Congress Cataloging-in-Publication number: Requested
ISBN: (print) 978-1-68481-887-7, (ebook) 978-1-68481-888-4
BISAC category code: SEL045000 SELF-HELP / Journaling

Introduction

I was tired, stressed out, and I knew it was time for a break. My eyes kept closing, and the words I had studied and reread for my upcoming finals for what felt like the hundredth time were blurring together on the page and in my head.

Luckily, my university's main library was steps away from a lake. Despite the chilly air, I decided to take the lake path instead of walking through campus in hopes of clearing my head.

I wasn't expecting what happened next.

I stood frozen at the edge of the water, mesmerized by the sound. I was in awe of what I heard. Despite it being a sunny, spring day in Madison, Wisconsin, some of the lake's winter ice remained intact along the shoreline. The waves moved these ice chunks in a delicate dance, producing one of the most beautiful wind-chime-like sounds I've ever heard. I felt frozen in time, not wanting this miraculous moment to end. Kneeling down by the water's edge to soak in the sound, I felt a sense of calm, peace, and connection. More than twenty years later, I can still picture where I was standing and hear the ice orchestra in my head. That moment made a lasting impression on me, and I found myself seeking and appreciating more of these magical micro moments, or glimmers, over the years.

As a busy mom of six, I admit that it can be challenging to step out of the daily grind and set aside the constant stream of distractions available at our fingertips long enough to notice tiny glimmers of joy. I promise, when you do stop and smell the roses, the changes in your life will be palpable.

Can one minute a day actually improve your well-being? The short answer is yes. Don't underestimate the power of a small moment in time. If you allow yourself to experience the joy a glimmer brings for at least one minute each day of the year, you'll have given your nervous system 365 opportunities to come back into regulation. Tiny sparks of joy that accumulate over time will positively affect your health and can permanently alter your nervous system.

A double rainbow in Paris. Stunning tulips at the Keukenhof gardens. The feeling of one of my babies burrowed into my shoulder. Reflections off Mirror Lake at Yosemite National Park. Watching the sun dance like diamonds on the water. Sunsets that paint the sky in magnificent rainbow hues. Tight hugs that last an extra ten seconds. These are just a few of the glimmer moments that spark joy and safety and keep me searching for more ways to bring joy into my life. Life can begin to feel like it's slipping by. This is why grounding yourself in glimmer moments helps your life feel more satisfying, peaceful, and meaningful. Finding these small moments of joy really does feel like one of the best small ways to incrementally improve your health, increase connection to yourself and others, and spend more of your time grounded in the present moment. As we age, finding these small moments can have just as big an impact on our mental health as more monumental events of our youth, like extravagant trips, career achievements, or starting a family.

Gratitude and Glimmers

People get happiness wrong. We think it's about external circumstances (more money, a better job, etc.). But true happiness comes from our connection with others, our ability to be present in the moment, helping others, having a sense of purpose, practicing self-compassion and, of course, gratitude. It's true that 50 percent of your baseline level of happiness is determined by your genetics, but research in positive psychology from Sonja Lyubomirsky, Kennon M. Sheldon, and David Schkade shows that you can raise that baseline by 5–15 percent by making small but consistent changes in just minutes a day.

By both incorporating a daily gratitude practice and being intentional about finding glimmers throughout your day, this dynamic duo can substantially increase your overall happiness.

What Is Gratitude?

Gratitude is a feeling of thanks or appreciation for people, things, experiences, life circumstances, events, animals, or natural wonders that bring joy into your life. When you recognize others and express thanks, it helps you lift your mood and spirits by focusing on the positive aspects of your life. Counting your blessings is a way to improve your happiness, relationships, resilience, and health.

What Are Glimmers?

According to Deb Dana, in her book *The Polyvagal Theory in Therapy*, glimmers are the opposite of triggers and can help you regulate your nervous system and remain calm. Through repeated exposure to and awareness of glimmers, you can actually alter your nervous system and improve your health. Acknowledging glimmers teaches your body the important skill of holding dysregulation and regulation at the same time. A glimmer can be something as simple as noticing a heart-shaped rock, hearing your favorite song on the radio, noticing a butterfly while walking outside, or appreciating the smell of fresh-baked bread at the bakery.

How to Use This Journal

Each page features space to write five things you are grateful for and five glimmers you experienced during the day, plus a prompt to help you discover future glimmers. Studies show that repeated exposure to and awareness of both gratitude and glimmers can significantly alter your nervous system and improve your overall health. Creating this consistent habit will help improve your overall sense of enjoyment, fulfillment, and satisfaction.

The prompts at the bottom of each page are all intended to get you diving deeper into memories and emotions and experiences, and the things that do help increase your happiness. The goal is for you to experience a prompt and have it help you keep in mind what your future glimmers could be. For example, if a question asks you to recall a favorite memory, this will hopefully get you thinking about how you can experience that same joy in the future, but from a new experience. The more you can remind yourself to stay fully present through your interactions with others, your experiences, and your daily routine, the happier you'll become over time. And your prompt for the day may be just what you need to shake things up and focus on the things that truly matter most.

1. What did you do for fun as a kid? What did you secretly love doing when you were younger? What could you incorporate into your day tomorrow to give you that childlike sense of wonder and carefree fun?

Example Page

GRATITUDE

1. Calling an old friend for a five-minute conversation.
2. Trying a new recipe with garden fresh tomatoes.
3. Feeling fully recovered from a cold.
4. Listening to my child laugh.
5. Walking my dog on a new path.

GLIMMERS

1. Watching the sunset.
2. Catching a butterfly perched on a garden flower.
3. Matcha green tea with milk foam.
4. Walking barefoot in the grass.
5. An end-of-day hug.

Take some time to write out a "best of" list. Make a gratitude notecard (or use this space) where you write five things you're most grateful for. Over the next four weeks, try adding one to two people, places, or things you appreciate once a week. Every day, look at this list for three minutes and soak in the gratitude you feel when you recount your blessings.

DATE

GRATITUDE	GLIMMERS
1	1
2	2
3	3
4	4
5	5

2. Did you have a favorite board game as a child? What was it, and why did you love it? When was the last time you played a game? Is there a game you've been wanting to learn to play?

DATE

GRATITUDE	GLIMMERS
1	1
2	2
3	3
4	4
5	5

3. If you could allow your imagination time to run wild, what would your ideal future look like? Where would you live? What kind of work or volunteering would you be doing? Who would you surround yourself with? What would your daily rhythm look like? Share your dreams below.

DATE

GRATITUDE	GLIMMERS
1	1
2	2
3	3
4	4
5	5

4. Describe one of the best meals you've ever had. Make a list of the textures and flavors of the food, and what made it so delicious.

DATE

GRATITUDE	GLIMMERS
1	1
2	2
3	3
4	4
5	5

5. Do you have a favorite memory of sharing a meal with friends or family?

DATE

GRATITUDE	GLIMMERS
1	1
2	2
3	3
4	4
5	5

6. When was the last time you stepped outside and looked up at the moon or the stars? Describe what you saw and how you felt.

DATE

GRATITUDE	GLIMMERS
1	1
2	2
3	3
4	4
5	5

7. If you could have your best day tomorrow, what would you do to make it great? What would you prioritize? Who or what would get your attention? Make a list of three to five things that would make your day memorable in small or big ways.

DATE

GRATITUDE	GLIMMERS
1	1
2	2
3	3
4	4
5	5

8. What's your favorite memory of being outdoors? When was the last time you spent time outdoors without an agenda?

DATE

GRATITUDE	GLIMMERS
1	1
2	2
3	3
4	4
5	5

9. What clever ways can you bring outdoor elements into your home as a way to promote your connection to nature and the outside world? A nature screensaver on your computer, a framed photograph or landscape painting, plants, or even natural elements like rocks and wood can give you a happy boost. List a few things you can bring into your home to connect more to the outdoor elements.

DATE

GRATITUDE	GLIMMERS
1	1
2	2
3	3
4	4
5	5

10. When was the last time you reached for your phone? One minute ago, ten minutes ago, an hour ago? Why did you reach for your phone? Was it to make a phone call? Scroll social media? Check your email? What else could you be doing instead? Write down some alternatives.

DATE

GRATITUDE	GLIMMERS
1	1
2	2
3	3
4	4
5	5

11. What song makes you want to turn your broom handle into a microphone and sing karaoke, and why?

DATE

GRATITUDE	GLIMMERS
1	1
2	2
3	3
4	4
5	5

12. Use the 5-4-3-2-1 grounding method anytime you're feeling anxious or simply want to be more present. What are five things you see? What are four things you can feel on your body or touch? What are three things you hear? What are two things you can smell, and what's one thing you can taste? Share how this made you feel below.

DATE

GRATITUDE	GLIMMERS
1	1
2	2
3	3
4	4
5	5

13. When was the last time you were quiet and still enough to hear nature sounds around you? Do you have a favorite place you like to experience nature?

DATE

GRATITUDE	GLIMMERS
1	1
2	2
3	3
4	4
5	5

14. Did you have a favorite blanket when you were a kid? Do you have one now? What is it about it (or them) that you love? Is it the color, the fabric, a memory it holds?
    Describe your blanket here.

DATE

GRATITUDE	GLIMMERS
1	1
2	2
3	3
4	4
5	5

15. Experiencing new and novel adventures helps you feel happier, less stressed, and more creative, and can improve your immunity. What can you put in your calendar to look forward to in the near future?

DATE

GRATITUDE	GLIMMERS
1	1
2	2
3	3
4	4
5	5

16. It sounds morbid, but writing your own obituary can be a fascinating exercise to discover where you want to focus your energy in your life, how you want to be remembered, and what dreams you still have left to achieve. Take time to write out how you envision your legacy. What would give your story a happy ending? Ask questions like: "*How do I want to be remembered by friends and family? What mark do I want to leave on other people's lives? What things brought me joy?*"

DATE

GRATITUDE	GLIMMERS
1	1
2	2
3	3
4	4
5	5

17. Everything doesn't always happen for a reason. Sometimes things—bad things—happen and it's up to us to find meaning from the experience, recognize a way we changed, or find a way we were able to grow because of what happened. We can go through things or grow through things. What are you going through right now that is causing you to grow in new and unexpected ways?

DATE

GRATITUDE	GLIMMERS
1	1
2	2
3	3
4	4
5	5

18. Have you sat at the water's edge and been mesmerized by watching the ebb and flow of the tide, or waves crashing against the shore, or a rushing river weaving over rocks and under bridges? Describe your favorite water scene and the feelings you experienced because of it.

DATE

GRATITUDE	GLIMMERS
1	1
2	2
3	3
4	4
5	5

19. When was the last time you planned an adventure? Going on adventures isn't just about ticking off items on your bucket list. Experiencing new and novel adventures helps you feel happier, less stressed, and more creative, and can improve your immunity. Look at a map and give yourself five minutes to write out a list of adventures, both near and far, that you've been wanting to explore. Make time to add one adventure to your calendar this month.

DATE

GRATITUDE

1

2

3

4

5

GLIMMERS

1

2

3

4

5

20. What activity have you always wanted to try? What would it take for you to finally try it?

DATE

GRATITUDE	GLIMMERS
1	1
2	2
3	3
4	4
5	5

21. What is a food you've always been curious to try? What would it take for you to finally try it?

DATE

GRATITUDE	GLIMMERS
1	1
2	2
3	3
4	4
5	5

22. Is there something or somewhere in your town that you haven't explored, but have been wanting to? What is it, and what would it take for you to plan your adventure?

DATE

GRATITUDE	GLIMMERS
1	1
2	2
3	3
4	4
5	5

23. When was the last time you struck up a conversation with a complete stranger? Describe where it was and how it went. Where can you find opportunities in your day to connect with people you don't know?

DATE

GRATITUDE	GLIMMERS
1	1
2	2
3	3
4	4
5	5

24. Do you have a favorite story from your childhood? Describe it in detail, using as many of your five senses as possible.

DATE

GRATITUDE	GLIMMERS
1	1
2	2
3	3
4	4
5	5

25. Is there a funny story you love to tell again and again? Describe it below.

DATE

GRATITUDE	GLIMMERS
1	1
2	2
3	3
4	4
5	5

26. Do you ever have moments when it feels like everything else just falls away and you're truly present in the moment? Have there been times that were so good you wished you could freeze time or hit the pause button? Describe one of those experiences here.

DATE

GRATITUDE	GLIMMERS
1	1
2	2
3	3
4	4
5	5

27. Do you have a favorite scent? Maybe it's fresh florals, or baked goods, or something else altogether. Describe that scent and what you like best about it. Is there a special memory you have in connection with that scent? If so, write that down as well.

DATE

GRATITUDE	GLIMMERS
1	1
2	2
3	3
4	4
5	5

28. Smiles naturally boost our mood, reduce pain, decrease our stress, and make us feel good. A smile, even if you don't feel happy, can even trick your brain into having more positive emotions. When was the last time you made someone smile?

DATE

GRATITUDE	GLIMMERS
1	1
2	2
3	3
4	4
5	5

29. The term "pluviophile" refers to someone who finds peace and joy in rain. Have you ever let yourself get soaked in the rain? Did you love the fun of splashing in puddles after a rainstorm in your childhood? Describe the last time you remember enjoying the rain.

DATE

GRATITUDE	GLIMMERS
1	1
2	2
3	3
4	4
5	5

30. When was the last time you had a good cry? How did it feel?

DATE

GRATITUDE	GLIMMERS
1	1
2	2
3	3
4	4
5	5

31. Laughing can stimulate your immune system and internal organs, increase oxygenating airflow into the body, increase the release of endorphins in the brain, and lower blood pressure. What's your favorite way to get a guaranteed laugh?

DATE

GRATITUDE	GLIMMERS
1	1
2	2
3	3
4	4
5	5

32. What's something you can do in less than three minutes that will start your day off with a small win? Write it down, claim it, and try it tomorrow.

DATE

GRATITUDE	GLIMMERS
1	1
2	2
3	3
4	4
5	5

33. How often do you reach out to loved ones, letting them know how much they mean to you? Who could you reach out to tomorrow and share a message of gratitude?

DATE

GRATITUDE	GLIMMERS
1	1
2	2
3	3
4	4
5	5

34. When was the last time you got a piece of fun snail mail? Describe it and how it made you feel.

DATE

GRATITUDE	GLIMMERS
1	1
2	2
3	3
4	4
5	5

35. When was the last time you sent a piece of snail mail? Who was it addressed to and how did it make you feel?

DATE

GRATITUDE	GLIMMERS
1	1
2	2
3	3
4	4
5	5

36. When was the last time you had an impromptu dance party? What songs did you choose? How did it make you feel?

DATE

GRATITUDE	GLIMMERS
1	1
2	2
3	3
4	4
5	5

37. Who do you know who gives the best hugs? Who do you look forward to seeing because you know you'll get a big squeeze? Who can you share one with this week?

DATE

GRATITUDE	GLIMMERS
1	1
2	2
3	3
4	4
5	5

38. Is there a period of your day that's screen-free? If yes, describe how that makes you feel. If not, do you want to start incorporating more screen-free time into your day, and if so, why?

DATE

GRATITUDE	GLIMMERS
1	1
2	2
3	3
4	4
5	5

39. When was the last time you received a compliment and really allowed yourself to take in the kindness?

DATE

GRATITUDE	GLIMMERS
1	1
2	2
3	3
4	4
5	5

40. When was the last time you shared a compliment with someone else? Did you notice how giving the compliment helped you linger in the present moment a little longer? Describe how giving the compliment made you feel.

DATE

GRATITUDE	GLIMMERS
1	1
2	2
3	3
4	4
5	5

41. What would make tomorrow feel like a fresh start?

DATE

GRATITUDE	GLIMMERS
1	1
2	2
3	3
4	4
5	5

42. Did you have a favorite song as a child? What was it, and why did you love it?

DATE

GRATITUDE	GLIMMERS
1	1
2	2
3	3
4	4
5	5

43. Describe songs that make you feel the following moods:

Happy:

Sad:

Peaceful:

Angry:

Excited:

Scared:

DATE

GRATITUDE	GLIMMERS
1	1
2	2
3	3
4	4
5	5

44. What's your favorite climate and why? How can you spend more time in the temperature and environment you love?

DATE

GRATITUDE	GLIMMERS
1	1
2	2
3	3
4	4
5	5

45. Did you have a favorite stuffed animal as a child? Do you still have your favorite cuddly animal today? How does it make you feel?

DATE

GRATITUDE	GLIMMERS
1	1
2	2
3	3
4	4
5	5

46. *Sigh.* Everyone can relate to the feeling behind an audible sigh. Creating audible sounds from your body, like a sigh, is actually a sign that your body is looking for nervous system regulation and is a proven way to decrease stress. Think back to your sighs from today and what triggered them.

DATE

GRATITUDE	GLIMMERS
1	1
2	2
3	3
4	4
5	5

47. What are three things that went well today? Can you challenge yourself to remember even small things that went well, even if today didn't go your way?

DATE

GRATITUDE	GLIMMERS
1	1
2	2
3	3
4	4
5	5

48. What is the one thing you are most excited about in your life right now?

DATE

GRATITUDE	GLIMMERS
1	1
2	2
3	3
4	4
5	5

49. Take a moment today to watch the sunset, or simply imagine it in your mind's eye. As you do, reflect on how the day went—what brought you joy, what challenged you, and how you might approach tomorrow differently. How can creating a daily "golden hour" ritual help you find stillness and peace?

DATE

GRATITUDE	GLIMMERS
1	1
2	2
3	3
4	4
5	5

50. When was the last time you went outside and played in the snow? How can you bring that same sense of wonder and playfulness into your life today, even if there's no snow? What simple activity could help you reconnect with that peaceful, serene joy?

DATE

GRATITUDE	GLIMMERS
1	1
2	2
3	3
4	4
5	5

51. Think of three people in your life you could compliment tomorrow. What genuine and thoughtful things can you say to brighten their day? How do you feel when you pause to notice the good in others?

DATE

GRATITUDE	GLIMMERS
1	1
2	2
3	3
4	4
5	5

52. What warm foods bring you comfort, or remind you of being cared for as a child? Plan a moment this week to enjoy or make something warm that nourishes both your body and spirit. How does this act of self-care make you feel?

DATE

GRATITUDE	GLIMMERS
1	1
2	2
3	3
4	4
5	5

53. Think of a time when you saw sunlight glimmering on water and felt captivated by its beauty. During your day, try noticing something that captures your attention in the same way and reminds you of the beauty all around you.

DATE

GRATITUDE	GLIMMERS
1	1
2	2
3	3
4	4
5	5

54. Reflect on the bond between humans and dogs. If you have a dog, how can you show extra gratitude for their companionship? If not, how might you spend time with a four-legged friend to experience the joy and unconditional love they bring?

DATE

GRATITUDE	GLIMMERS
1	1
2	2
3	3
4	4
5	5

55. What creative activities brought you joy as a child? Maybe it was doodling, painting, making up stories, or building with blocks. What are some ways you can bring that same playful creativity into your life now?

DATE

GRATITUDE	GLIMMERS
1	1
2	2
3	3
4	4
5	5

56. When was the last time you stepped outside and simply looked up at the vast sky? Reflect on how this perspective can shift your mood and help you feel part of something greater than yourself. What stressors could you let go of by appreciating the world's enormity?

DATE

GRATITUDE	GLIMMERS
1	1
2	2
3	3
4	4
5	5

57. What scents bring you comfort, joy, or a sense of calm? Plan to intentionally add one of these scents into your day—whether through candles, fresh cookies, or flowers. How does the smell affect your mood, or help you feel grounded?

DATE

GRATITUDE	GLIMMERS
1	1
2	2
3	3
4	4
5	5

58. Look for repeating patterns and fractals in nature, like those found in leaf veins, snowflakes, succulents, or tree branches. Spend a couple of minutes observing these patterns and notice how you feel. How might noticing the small details in the world around you help you feel calmer and more connected?

DATE

GRATITUDE	GLIMMERS
1	1
2	2
3	3
4	4
5	5

59. Did you have a favorite stuffed animal or comfort item as a child? Do you remember it bringing you a sense of security or calm? If you could choose a comfort object today, what would it be and why? You're never too old for a fuzzy friend, and it just might improve your ability to fall asleep.

DATE

GRATITUDE	GLIMMERS
1	1
2	2
3	3
4	4
5	5

60. Reflect on your current sleep habits. Are you prioritizing rest as much as your body needs? What small changes—like investing in cozy pajamas or starting a calming bedtime ritual—could help you create a more restful environment?

DATE

GRATITUDE	GLIMMERS
1	1
2	2
3	3
4	4
5	5

61. Tonight, consider a simple pre-sleep meditation. As you lie in bed, breathe in for a count of four, hold your breath for four, breathe out for four, and hold again for four. How does it feel to slow down and be present with your breath before sleep?

DATE

GRATITUDE	GLIMMERS
1	1
2	2
3	3
4	4
5	5

62. What memories do you have of being barefoot in nature—squishing your toes in the mud, walking in the grass, or digging in the sand? Reflect on how you could incorporate grounding practices into your life today. How might reconnecting with the earth bring you a sense of healing or peace?

DATE

GRATITUDE	GLIMMERS
1	1
2	2
3	3
4	4
5	5

63. What do you notice when you sit quietly in the sun, or watch clouds drift by? Imagine attaching a sticky thought or worry to a passing cloud—how does it feel to let it float away?

DATE

GRATITUDE	GLIMMERS
1	1
2	2
3	3
4	4
5	5

64. Can you actively notice and savor small glimmers of joy or gratitude you find throughout your day? If you started your day with five pennies in your pocket to represent moments of gratitude, what moments would move them to the other pocket? Write about how acknowledging these moments changes your outlook.

DATE

GRATITUDE	GLIMMERS
1	1
2	2
3	3
4	4
5	5

65. Do you have a small token—like a stone, shell, or crystal—that evokes a special memory or connection? How might carrying it with you bring you comfort or joy during the day? Reflect on how such small treasures can ground and inspire you.

DATE

GRATITUDE	GLIMMERS
1	1
2	2
3	3
4	4
5	5

66. When was the last time you sat quietly watching the flickering light of a candle? Reflect on how candles and the movement of their flame, or their scent, ignites a sense of calm and self-awareness. What type of candlelight ritual could bring you peace in your daily life?

DATE

GRATITUDE	GLIMMERS
1	1
2	2
3	3
4	4
5	5

67. When was the last time you felt a sense of comfort from something warm, like a bath, a hot drink, or a weighted blanket? How do these physical comforts help when you're feeling lonely or stressed? Reflect on how you might create moments of warmth for yourself.

DATE

GRATITUDE

1

2

3

4

5

GLIMMERS

1

2

3

4

5

68. Think of a loved one's voice that brings you comfort. What is it about their voice that soothes or inspires you? How could hearing their voice help you through a difficult moment? Reflect on the power of connection, even through a voicemail or memory.

DATE

GRATITUDE	GLIMMERS
1	1
2	2
3	3
4	4
5	5

69. What is your favorite drink on a cold or hot day, and why does it bring you comfort? Reflect on how the warmth of tea or the coolness of lemonade can shift your mood. What could you add to your next beverage to make it feel extra special?

DATE

GRATITUDE

1

2

3

4

5

GLIMMERS

1

2

3

4

5

70. What's a spice or herb you've enjoyed recently, or one you'd like to experiment with? How do certain tastes or smells evoke memories or bring comfort? Reflect on how you might wake up your senses with new flavors or scents.

DATE

GRATITUDE	GLIMMERS
1	1
2	2
3	3
4	4
5	5

71. What video, show, or clip always makes you laugh or brings you joy? How could you build a "joy library" to turn to when you need a boost?

DATE

GRATITUDE	GLIMMERS
1	1
2	2
3	3
4	4
5	5

72. What's your go-to piece of clothing for comfort, and how does it make you feel? How might investing in soft, cozy fabrics and prioritizing comfort improve your mood, your sleep, or your daily life?

DATE

GRATITUDE	GLIMMERS
1	1
2	2
3	3
4	4
5	5

73. Brigid Schulte, author of *Overwhelmed: How to Work, Love & Play When No One Has the Time*, coined the term "time confetti," which describes small moments of free time seen as opportunities to do something meaningful as opposed to doing nothing. What are five small but meaningful things you could do in a five-minute window? How does viewing short bursts of time as valuable change your perspective?

DATE

GRATITUDE	GLIMMERS
1	1
2	2
3	3
4	4
5	5

74. What were your three roses (good moments), one bud (something you're looking forward to), and one thorn (a challenge) from today? Reflect on how sharing or writing about these can foster connection and self-awareness.

DATE

GRATITUDE	GLIMMERS
1	1
2	2
3	3
4	4
5	5

75. What area of your life has been neglected lately, and how could you nurture it this week? Reflect on what matters most to you right now. What small action can you take to bring yourself closer to what's truly important?

DATE

GRATITUDE	GLIMMERS
1	1
2	2
3	3
4	4
5	5

76. What are five small acts of kindness you could do for others this week? Reflect on how these acts, whether big or small, could ripple out to create more positivity. How can you plan for intentional kindness this week? How do you anticipate it will make you feel?

DATE

GRATITUDE	GLIMMERS
1	1
2	2
3	3
4	4
5	5

77. What's a small, ridiculously easy goal you could set for yourself tomorrow—something so tiny you couldn't possibly fail? Reflect on how consistent, small improvements might add up over time. What's one way you can celebrate even the smallest success?

DATE

GRATITUDE	GLIMMERS
1	1
2	2
3	3
4	4
5	5

78. Make a list of the five people you spend the most time with. How do these relationships make you feel—energized, inspired, or drained? Based on your reflections, who do you want to spend more time with, and how might you gracefully distance yourself from relationships that no longer serve you?

DATE

GRATITUDE	GLIMMERS
1	1
2	2
3	3
4	4
5	5

79. Look around your home and observe the objects in your space. Are there items that no longer bring you joy or peace? What steps can you take to simplify your environment and create a home filled with things that truly inspire you?

DATE

GRATITUDE	GLIMMERS
1	1
2	2
3	3
4	4
5	5

80. Ground yourself in the present moment with the 5-4-3-2-1 technique: name five things you see, four you feel, three you hear, two you smell, and one you taste. What new details about your surroundings or sensations did you notice that you've overlooked before? How can you incorporate this simple practice into your daily life, especially during stressful times?

DATE

GRATITUDE	GLIMMERS
1	1
2	2
3	3
4	4
5	5

81. Accept that your to-do list will never truly be finished. With this in mind, what people, projects, or tasks are most deserving of your time today? What can you let go of to create more balance and peace in your day?

DATE

GRATITUDE	GLIMMERS
1	1
2	2
3	3
4	4
5	5

82. Reflect on ways you can step outside your daily grind by helping others. Who could benefit from your time, energy, or kindness this week? How might volunteering or supporting a cause close to your heart bring you a renewed sense of purpose or gratitude?

DATE

GRATITUDE	GLIMMERS
1	1
2	2
3	3
4	4
5	5

83. Think of a challenging situation where the idea that "everything happens for a reason" didn't resonate. How could you find meaning or growth from this experience? What's one way you can reframe your story to bring empowerment or closure?

DATE

GRATITUDE	GLIMMERS
1	1
2	2
3	3
4	4
5	5

84. How do you treat yourself compared to the way you treat your loved ones? What would nurturing yourself look like, and how can you ensure your needs are met?

DATE

GRATITUDE	GLIMMERS
1	1
2	2
3	3
4	4
5	5

85. Research shows that up to 40 percent of your happiness is within your control. What's one small, meaningful step you can take this week—spending time with loved ones, moving your body, being in the present moment, helping others, practicing self-kindness, or practicing gratitude—to improve your overall happiness?

DATE

GRATITUDE	GLIMMERS
1	1
2	2
3	3
4	4
5	5

86. Reflect on how you handle situations that don't go as planned. Can you find beauty in something "perfectly imperfect" that happened today? How might this perspective help you embrace life's silver linings?

DATE

GRATITUDE	GLIMMERS
1	1
2	2
3	3
4	4
5	5

87. Imagine your life as a jar filled with golf balls, pebbles, and sand, where the golf balls represent your biggest priorities, like health, family, and passions. What are your "golf balls," and how can you protect them from getting buried under the smaller, insignificant sand and pebbles?

DATE

GRATITUDE	GLIMMERS
1	1
2	2
3	3
4	4
5	5

88. What experience have you been postponing, and how could you share it with someone meaningful to you? Plan an outing, activity, or trip that focuses on creating lasting memories over material gains.

DATE

GRATITUDE	GLIMMERS
1	1
2	2
3	3
4	4
5	5

89. What moments in your life have stopped you in your tracks and filled you with awe? Think about a time you marveled at something in nature, like a flower, a waterfall, or a spiderweb. Write about how you can cultivate more moments of awe in your daily life, perhaps through travel, time in nature, or simply paying closer attention to the world around you.

DATE

GRATITUDE

1

2

3

4

5

GLIMMERS

1

2

3

4

5

90. When have you felt like time was slipping through your fingers? Reflect on how monotony or routine might make time feel like a blur. Write about one way you can break up your usual routine or create novelty this week—whether it's planning something exciting or simply taking a new route or trying a new activity.

DATE

GRATITUDE	GLIMMERS
1	1
2	2
3	3
4	4
5	5

91. Think about a recent time you experienced happiness or joy. Were you able to fully appreciate the moment? Write about how you can practice stopping and acknowledging that "This is a happy moment" and savor all the details that make it special.

DATE

GRATITUDE

1

2

3

4

5

GLIMMERS

1

2

3

4

5

92. Who in your life has ever "made your day"? Reflect on how their kindness or positivity impacted you and decide to be a "daymaker" for someone you know and love.

DATE

GRATITUDE	GLIMMERS
1	1
2	2
3	3
4	4
5	5

93. Write about the three most important things you could focus on tomorrow that align with your long-term goals or would give you the greatest sense of accomplishment. How can prioritizing these help you feel more productive and at peace?

DATE

GRATITUDE	GLIMMERS
1	1
2	2
3	3
4	4
5	5

94. Imagine you're looking back on your life. What three things would you want to have accomplished to feel fulfilled and content? Reflect on three small steps you can take this week to move closer to those goals. How you can commit to consistently making progress?

DATE

GRATITUDE	GLIMMERS
1	1
2	2
3	3
4	4
5	5

95. Who was your best teacher or role model? What advice did they give you that has stuck with you over the years?

DATE

GRATITUDE	GLIMMERS
1	1
2	2
3	3
4	4
5	5

96. Are you happy with your life? Are you happy in your life? Reflect on the distinction between these two questions. Where do you want to focus your attention this week?

DATE

GRATITUDE	GLIMMERS
1	1
2	2
3	3
4	4
5	5

97. Practice self-compassion today. Remember a difficult moment you experienced recently and remind yourself that sometimes life is hard. Recognize your feelings as valid and assure yourself that someone else is going through the same or similar situation right now. Can you talk to yourself the way you'd advise a friend in the same situation?

DATE

GRATITUDE	GLIMMERS
1	1
2	2
3	3
4	4
5	5

98. If you were given twenty-four hours to live, what would your final day look like? Who would you be with? What would you eat? Where would you go? What would you do?

DATE

GRATITUDE	GLIMMERS
1	1
2	2
3	3
4	4
5	5

99. Who do you most admire? Why? Take time to write that person a letter of thanks and praise. Consider making this gratitude letter a monthly practice.

DATE

GRATITUDE

1

2

3

4

5

GLIMMERS

1

2

3

4

5

100. What's the most memorable concert or show you ever attended? What event could you plan to attend in the coming months or year?

Resources

Podcasts

The Mel Robbins Podcast

The Happiness Lab with Dr. Laurie Santos

Ten Percent Happier with Dan Harris and Tara Brach

Everything Happens with Kate Bowler

Ask Lisa: The Psychology of Parenting with Lisa Damour

Raising Good Humans with Dr. Aliza Pressman

Work Life with Adam Grant

Unlocking Us with Brené Brown

Happier with Gretchen Rubin

Hidden Brain with Shankar Vedantam

Books

The How of Happiness: A New Approach to Getting the Life You Want by Sonja Lyubomirsky

The Good Life: Lessons from the World's Longest Scientific Study of Happiness by Robert Waldinger, MD, and Marc Schulz, PhD

From Strength to Strength: Finding Success, Happiness and Deep Purpose in the Second Half of Life by Arthur C. Brooks

Grit: The Power of Passion and Perseverance by Angela Duckworth

The Happiness Trap by Russ Harris

Authentic Happiness by Martin E. P. Seligman, PhD

Happier Hour by Cassie Holms

24/6: The Power of Unplugging by Tiffany Shlain

Chatter: The Voice in Our Head, Why It Matters, and How to Harness It by Ethan Kross

Four Thousand Weeks: Time Management for Mortals by Oliver Burkeman

The Let Them Theory: The Life-Changing Tool That Millions of People Can't Stop Talking About by Mel Robbins

Tiny Habits by B. J. Fogg, PhD

The Happiness Advantage: The Seven Principles of Positive Psychology That Fuel Success and Performance at Work by Shawn Achor

The Artist's Way by Julia Cameron

Happier: Learn the Secrets to Daily Joy and Lasting Fulfillment by Tal Ben-Shahar

The Midnight Library by Matt Haig

How to Be Enough by Ellen Hendriksen

When Things Fall Apart: Heart Advice for Difficult Times by Pema Chodron

Buy Back Your Time by Dan Martell

The Happiness Hypothesis: Finding Modern Truth in Ancient Wisdom by Jonathan Haidt

About the Author

Andrea Dow has more than fifteen years of experience as a certified personal trainer, Pilates instructor, yoga teacher, and health coach. Andrea brings a wealth of expertise and compassion to her transformative work.

Today, Andrea serves as a certified weight coach as well as a yoga and Pilates teacher, offering a guiding hand to individuals seeking liberation from chronic dieting and negative body image. Through her compassionate coaching and evidence-based techniques, she empowers her clients to rewire their attitudes, cultivate self-love, and embrace a lifestyle grounded in health and vitality. Her work has been featured online on Scary Mommy, Byrdie, Positively Positive, and Tiny Buddha. She is also the author of *Raising Anti-Diet Kids: A Parent's Actionable Guide to Ditch Diets and Cultivate Body Respect.*

Aside from her professional accomplishments, Andrea is also a mom of six and finds joy in nurturing her large family and embarking on adventures around the globe. She is always searching for her next glimmer.

www.ingramcontent.com/pod-product-compliance
Lightning Source LLC
LaVergne TN
LVHW020639210826
846105LV00027B/366